# Cuddle Baby & Scuttle Bug

# My Fraternal Twins

For Leah and Lydia

From Mom, Dad,
Emily, and Claudia

I have twin girls,
they have my heart.

I love them the same,
But they are worlds apart.

I call one Cuddle Baby
And the other one Scuttle Bug.

They are two of a kind,
So sweet and so smart.

My twin girls are double love,
My Cuddle Baby and Scuttle Bug.

Cuddle Baby loves to hug,
And curious is my Scuttle Bug.

My Scuttle Bug scampers and scurries.
She rips and rambles and gets in a hurry.
Cuddle Baby creeps when she crawls,
Then curls up to get cozy and snug.

Cuddle Baby stays close by
Her mommy's and daddy's side.
She likes to play and make silly faces.
She lets daddy lift her high.

As long as Daddy is arm length away,
Cuddle Baby is never afraid.
She doesn't let mommy get away.
She sings "Hold me mommy,
hold me all day!"

Scuttle Bug shuttles by.
She goes and goes in the blink of an eye,
As far as her little legs flutter,
To new adventures for her to find.

Never slowing, never stopping,
Just an occasional hi!
Until she tires and finds Mommy or Daddy
To sing her a sweet lullaby.

Now Scuttle Bug is too tired to scuttle.
Her and Cuddle Baby look to each other.
They go get comfy with their blankies,
And in Mommy's and Daddy's love
they are covered.

With a final twin connection,
their fingers mingle,
Then Cuddle Baby and Scuttle Bug
Are off to play in a dream land
All bundled up in a twin snuggle.

If you enjoyed this title,
please leave a positive review on Amazon.
Thank you so much!

www.ingramcontent.com/pod-product-compliance
Lightning Source LLC
Chambersburg PA
CBHW041614120626
46551CB00002B/442